MW01140416

# KNOCK KNOCK
## JOKES FOR KIDS

365 Jokes for Each Day
(and Holiday) of the Year

**CIEL PUBLISHING**

# DID YOU KNOW?

Knock knock jokes are scientifically proven to increase the chances of a smile by 97.3%. A team of giggling researchers conducted a study, and their findings revealed that even the cheesiest knock knock joke has a remarkable ability to crack people up.

# TABLE OF CONTENTS

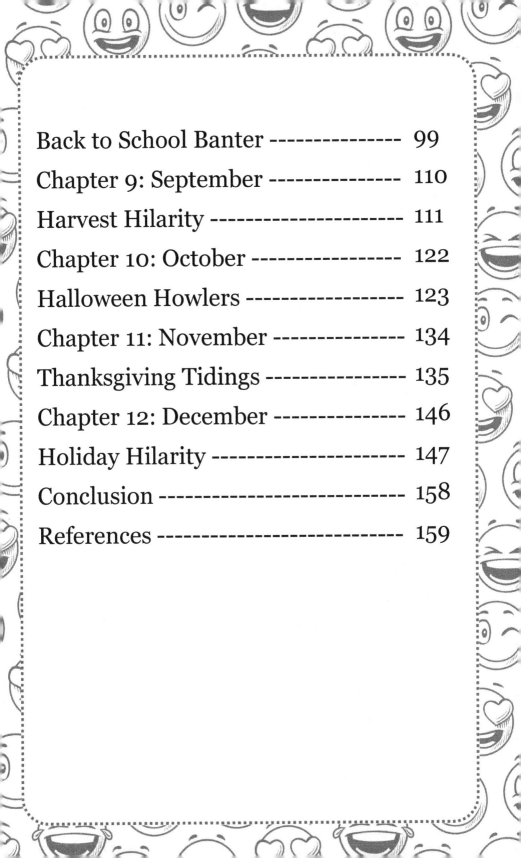

# INTRODUCTION

Knock, knock.

Who's there?

Joke book.

Joke book who?

This is a joke book for kids that you can spend hours on!

Specifically, this is a book of knock-knock jokes, which are some of the best jokes to tell. If you don't already know, here is how they work:

You say, "Knock, knock," as if you're knocking on somebody's door.

The other person has to say, "Who's there?"

You say a name or a word, such as, "Joe."

The other person replies, "Joe who?"

And then you deliver the punchline: "Joe-kes are very funny!"

That was a pun, a play on words. You made the other person think that there was someone named Joe knocking, but it was actually the first part of the word "jokes". You'll find that most, but not all, knock-knock jokes are puns. If you read this book by yourself, you may have to read some of the punchlines out loud to understand the gag.

Why is this one of the best kinds of jokes, do you ask? Because it involves two people: Someone needs to knock and someone needs to ask who's there. That makes it a fun activity for both the person telling the joke and the person hearing it. Most other kinds of jokes are just short stories where the audience's job is just to listen and then laugh at the end. Some jokes, such as, "Why did the chicken cross the road?" just need the listener to say, "I don't know, why?" and then immediately deliver the punchline. It's hard for people to bond with those jokes—but knock-knock jokes take both of you on a journey! It's not a long journey, but it's one where both people are more or less equally involved.

And how many knock-knock jokes can you find in this book? Literally a year's worth! This book contains almost as many knock-knock jokes as there are days in a year. We even divided them into months, for your convenience. Each chapter has jokes about the things we associate with each month of the year, plus a little fun fact about that month at the end of each chapter—because jokes are fun, but learning is fun too.

You can read this book by yourself or with someone else; The jokes will be funny either way, but we recommend you read them to someone—your parents, siblings, friends, or grandparents. It's a good bonding experience. Remember that when you knock on a door, it's always better to have someone you love opening it for you.

# DOWNLOAD YOUR FREE GIFT

Thank you for getting a copy of this book. As a token of my appreciation, I have a special gift for you and your young adventurers: a free ebook titled "**Super Interesting Facts and Trivia Questions for Kids.**"

Link: https://tinyurl.com/Super-Interesting-Facts

This interactive book is packed with fascinating facts and exciting trivia questions that will ignite your child's curiosity and love for the natural world. It's perfect for kids of all knowledge levels, with easy-to-understand language and engaging visuals.

To download your free ebook and continue this exciting journey, scan this QR code.

Together, let's make learning an unforgettable adventure!

# CHAPTER 1
## January

The first chapter of our book is, of course, about the first month of the year: January! It's also the coldest month of the year, so we filled this chapter with jokes about snow and all the fun you can have when it's chilly outside. And, as we promised in the introduction, there's a fun fact about January waiting for you at the end of the chapter!

"Knock, knock."
"Who's there?"
"Lenny."
"Lenny who?"
"Lenny in,
it's getting cold!"

# WINTER WACKINESS

**"Knock, knock."**
"Who's there?"
**"Abbey."**
"Abbey who?"
**"Abbey new year! "**

\*\*\*

**"Knock, knock."**
"Who's there?"
**"Anna."**
"Anna who?"
**"Anna-other year has started. "**

\*\*\*

**"Knock, knock."**
"Who's there?"
**"Bear."**
"Bear who?"
**"Brrr, it's cold outside!"**

**"Knock, knock."**

"Who's there?"

**"Candice."**

"Candice who?"

**"Candice door open, please? It's really cold out here! "**

\*\*\*

**"Knock, knock."**

"Who's there?"

**"Geddy."**

"Geddy who?"

**"Geddy your skis, we're going skiing!"**

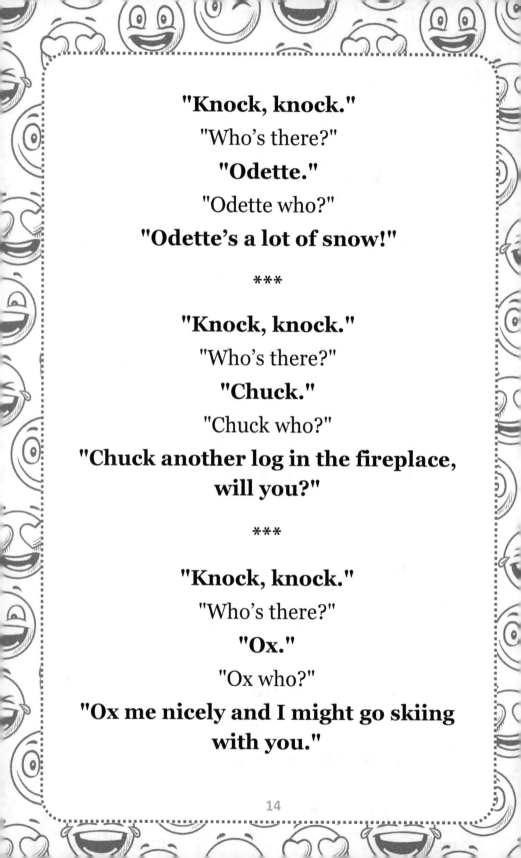

**"Knock, knock."**

"Who's there?"

**"Odette."**

"Odette who?"

**"Odette's a lot of snow!"**

\*\*\*

**"Knock, knock."**

"Who's there?"

**"Chuck."**

"Chuck who?"

**"Chuck another log in the fireplace, will you?"**

\*\*\*

**"Knock, knock."**

"Who's there?"

**"Ox."**

"Ox who?"

**"Ox me nicely and I might go skiing with you."**

**"Knock, knock."**

"Who's there?"

**"Scold."**

"Scold who?"

**"Scold outside!"**

\*\*\*

**"Knock, knock."**

"Who's there?"

**"Harmony."**

"Harmony who?"

**"Harmony times are we going to ski down this hill?"**

\*\*\*

**"Knock, knock."**

"Who's there?"

**"Cary."**

"Cary who?"

**"Cary me back home, I'm too tired from bobsledding!"**

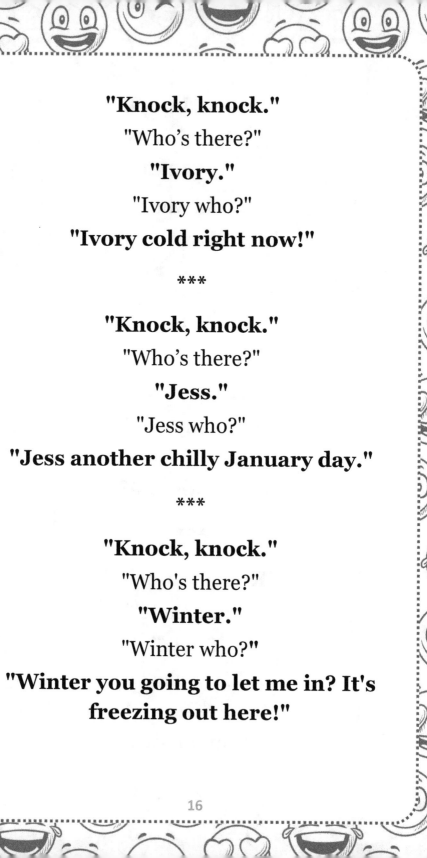

"Knock, knock."

"Who's there?"

**"Ivory."**

"Ivory who?"

**"Ivory cold right now!"**

\*\*\*

**"Knock, knock."**

"Who's there?"

**"Jess."**

"Jess who?"

**"Jess another chilly January day."**

\*\*\*

**"Knock, knock."**

"Who's there?"

**"Winter."**

"Winter who?"

**"Winter you going to let me in? It's freezing out here!"**

**"Knock, knock."**

"Who's there?"

**"Snow."**

"Snow who?"

**"Snow time like the present!"**

\*\*\*

**"Knock, knock."**

"Who's there?"

**"Ken."**

"Ken who?"

**"Ken I come in? It's cold out here! "**

\*\*\*

**"Knock, knock."**

"Who's there?"

**"Ivan."**

"Ivan who?"

**"Ivan to build a snowman."**

**"Knock, knock."**

"Who's there?"

**"Nose."**

"Nose who?"

**"I nose a great place where we can build a snowman."**

\*\*\*

**"Knock, knock."**

"Who's there?"

**"Pat."**

"Pat who?"

**"Pat your coat on, you'll catch a cold."**

\*\*\*

**"Knock, knock."**

"Who's there?"

**"Winter."**

"Winter who?"

**"Winter you going to stop with the cold weather, January?"**

**"Knock, knock."**

"Who's there?"

**"Les."**

"Les who?"

**"Les go build a snowman."**

\*\*\*

**"Knock, knock."**

"Who's there?"

**"Kara."**

"Kara who?"

**"Kar-rot to use as a nose for our snowman!"**

**"Knock, knock."**

"Who's there?"

**"Wilma."**

"Wilma who?"

**"Wilma hoodie be enough to keep me warm?"**

\*\*\*

**"Knock, knock."**

"Who's there?"

**"Dozen."**

"Dozen who?"

**"Dozen anyone want to go skiing? "**

\*\*\*

**"Knock, knock."**

"Who's there?"

**"Tyrone."**

"Tyrone who?"

**"Tyrone shoelaces and let's go play in the snow!"**

**"Knock, knock."**
"Who's there?"
**"Icing."**
"Icing who?"
**"Icing so loud that I can cause an avalanche."**

\*\*\*

**"Knock, knock."**
"Who's there?"
**"Omar."**
"Omar who?"
**"Omar goodness, it's cold out here."**

\*\*\*

**"Knock, knock."**
"Who's there?"
**"Irma."**
"Irma who?"
**"Irma go build a snowman."**

**"Knock, knock."**

"Who's there?"

**"Turner."**

"Turner who?"

**"Turner round and let's ski down this mountain."**

\*\*\*

**"Knock, knock."**

"Who's there?"

**"Your doorbell."**

"Your doorbell who?"

**"Your doorbell froze, that's why I knocked."**

## DID YOU KNOW?

January is named after the Roman god Janus. He was the god of doors, passageways, beginnings, and ends. When the old year ends, a new one begins, so the Romans named the first month of the year after him.

# CHAPTER 2
## February

February is both the shortest and the most romantic month of the year. That's because February 14th is Valentine's Day! So get cozy with your boo and have fun with these romance-related gags.

"**Knock, knock.**"
"Who's there?"
"**Jimmy.**"
"Jimmy who?"
"**Jimmy a kiss!**"

# VALENTINE'S DAY VIBES

**"Knock, knock."**
"Who's there?"
**"Will."**
"Will who?"
**"Will you be my Valentine?"**

\*\*\*

**"Knock, knock."**
"Who's there?"
**"Wooden shoe."**
"Wooden shoe who?"
**"Wooden shoe like some chocolate?"**

\*\*\*

**"Knock, knock."**
"Who's there?"
**"Howard."**
"Howard who?"
**"Howard you like to be my Valentine?"**

**"Knock, knock."**

"Who's there?"

**"Wire."**

"Wire who?"

**"Wire you so dang cute?"**

\*\*\*

**"Knock, knock."**

"Who's there?"

**"Wanda."**

"Wanda who?"

**"Wanda go out sometime?"**

\*\*\*

**"Knock, knock."**

"Who's there?"

**"Olive."**

"Olive who?"

**"Olive you!"**

**"Knock, knock."**
"Who's there?"
**"Nadia."**
"Nadia who?"
**"Nadia your head if you love me. "**

\*\*\*

**"Knock, knock."**
"Who's there?"
**"Keith."**
"Keith who?"
**"Keith me, my thweet."**

**"Knock, knock."**

"Who's there?"

**"Sam and Janice."**

"Sam and Janice who?"

**"Sam and Janice evening, you may see a stranger..."**

**\*\*\***

**"Knock, knock."**

"Who's there?"

**"Dewey."**

"Dewey who?"

**"Dewey make a cute couple or what?"**

**"Knock, knock."**

"Who's there?"

**"I love."**

"I love who?"

**"You tell me."**

\*\*\*

**"Knock, knock."**

"Who's there?"

**"Leonie."**

"Leonie who?"

**"Leonie one I love is you."**

\*\*\*

**"Knock, knock."**

"Who's there?"

**"De Niro."**

"De Niro who?"

**"De Niro you get, the happier I become."**

**"Knock, knock."**
"Who's there?"
**"Lena."**
"Lena who?"
**"Lena little closer to me."**

\*\*\*

**"Knock, knock."**
"Who's there?"
**"Major."**
"Major who?"
**"Major day with this box of chocolates, didn't I?"**

\*\*\*

**"Knock, knock."**
"Who's there?"
**"Arthur."**
"Arthur who?"
**"Arthur any chocolates left for me?"**

**"Knock, knock."**

"Who's there?"

**"Will and Hugh."**

"Will and Hugh who?"

**"Will Hugh marry me?"**

\*\*\*

**"Knock, knock."**

"Who's there?"

**"Pizza."**

"Pizza who?"

**"Pete's a great guy, you should go out with him."**

**"Knock, knock."**

"Who's there?"

**"Q."**

"Q who?"

**"Q-pid shot an arrow through my heart."**

\*\*\*

**"Knock, knock."**

"Who's there?"

**"Emma."**

"Emma who?"

**"Emma real fan of chocolate."**

\*\*\*

**"Knock, knock."**

"Who's there?"

**"Waddle."**

"Waddle who?"

**"Waddle I do if you won't go out with me?"**

**"Knock, knock."**

"Who's there?"

**"Gray."**

"Gray who?"

**"Gray-zy about you!"**

\*\*\*

**"Knock, knock."**

"Who's there?"

**"Yule."**

"Yule who?"

**"Yule be in my heart..."**

**"Knock, knock."**

"Who's there?"

**"Moira."**

"Moira who?"

**"The Moira I see you, the Moira I love you."**

\*\*\*

**"Knock, knock."**

"Who's there?"

**"Candice."**

"Candice who?"

**"Candice be love?"**

\*\*\*

**"Knock, knock."**

"Who's there?"

**"Pooch."**

"Pooch who?"

**"Pooch your arms around me!"**

**"Knock, knock."**

"Who's there?"

**"Mary."**

"Mary who?"

**"Mary me, will you?"**

## DID YOU KNOW?

Cupid is the name given by the Ancient Romans to the Greek god Eros. He was the god of love, represented as a young man with wings and holding a bow and arrow. When he shot people with a golden arrow, they would fall in love, but when he shot them with a lead-tipped arrow, their love would fade away.

# CHAPTER 3
## March

March is the beginning of spring, but in America and everywhere else that has people of Irish descent—like Ireland, for example—it is also a time to wear green and be joyful. Grab your shamrocks and enjoy these St. Patrick's Day jokes!

"Knock, knock."

"Who's there?"

"Sherwood."

"Sherwood who?"

"Sherwood like some Lucky Charms."

# ST. PATRICK'S SHENANIGANS

**"Knock, knock."**

"Who's there?"

**"Interrupting leprechaun."**

"Interrupting —"

**"Top o' the mornin' to ye!"**

\*\*\*

**"Knock, knock."**

"Who's there?"

**"Paddy."**

"Paddy who?"

**"Paddy O'Furniture!"**

**"Knock, knock."**

"Who's there?"

**"Radio."**

"Radio who?"

**"Radi-O'Donnell, the electronic Irishman!"**

\*\*\*

**"Knock, knock."**

"Who's there?"

**"Ada."**

"Ada who?"

**"Ada lot of Lucky Charms and now I'm gonna throw up."**

\*\*\*

**"Knock, knock."**

"Who's there?"

**"Manuel the Leprechaun."**

"Manuel the Leprechaun who?"

**"How many leprechauns named Manuel do you know?"**

"Knock, knock."

"Who's there?"

"Honeybee."

"Honeybee who?"

"Honey, be a dear and open the door."

\*\*\*

"Knock, knock."

"Who's there?"

"Warren."

"Warren who?"

"Warren any green for St. Patrick's Day?"

\*\*\*

"Knock, knock."

"Who's there?"

"Irish."

"Irish who?"

"Irish you would open the door."

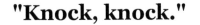

**"Knock, knock."**

"Who's there?"

**"Esme."**

"Esme who?"

**"Esme green shirt around here anywhere?"**

\*\*\*

**"Knock, knock."**

"Who's there?"

**"Noah."**

"Noah who?"

**"Noah any good Irish pubs around here?"**

"Knock, knock."

"Who's there?"

**"Don."**

"Don who?"

**"Don' be makin' fun of the Irish!"**

\*\*\*

"Knock, knock."

"Who's there?"

**"Handsome."**

"Handsome who?"

**"Handsome gold to me, I'm a leprechaun."**

\*\*\*

"Knock, knock."

"Who's there?"

**"Leprechaun knocking."**

"Leprechaun knocking who?"

**"Leprechaun knocking because he can't reach your doorbell!"**

**"Knock, knock."**

"Who's there?"

**"Irish."**

"Irish who?"

**"Irish stew in the name of the law."**

\*\*\*

**"Knock, knock."**

"Who's there?"

**"Ida."**

"Ida who?"

**"Ida know how this happened, but there's a leprechaun in my room."**

\*\*\*

**"Knock, knock."**

"Who's there?"

**"Alba."**

"Alba who?"

**"Alba at the pub if you need me."**

**"Knock, knock."**

"Who's there?"

**"Theresa."**

"Theresa who?"

**"Theresa leprechaun trying to steal my gold!"**

\*\*\*

**"Knock, knock."**

"Who's there?"

**"Luke."**

"Luke who?"

**"Luke-y Charms are a leprechaun's favorite cereal!"**

\*\*\*

**"Knock, knock."**

"Who's there?"

**"Abby."**

"Abby who?"

**"Abby good if you come to the St. Patrick's Day Parade with me."**

**"Knock, knock."**

"Who's there?"

**"Fungi."**

"Fungi who?"

**"Fungi here to join the party!"**

\*\*\*

**"Knock, knock."**

"Who's there?"

**"A mist."**

"A mist who?"

**"A mist you at the St. Patrick's Day party last night!"**

**"Knock, knock."**
"Who's there?"
**"Leprechaun who can't finish jokes."**
"Leprechaun who can't finish jokes who?"
**"Uh..."**

***

**"Knock, knock."**
"Who's there?"
**"Sam."**
"Sam who?"
**"Sam where over the rainbow..."**

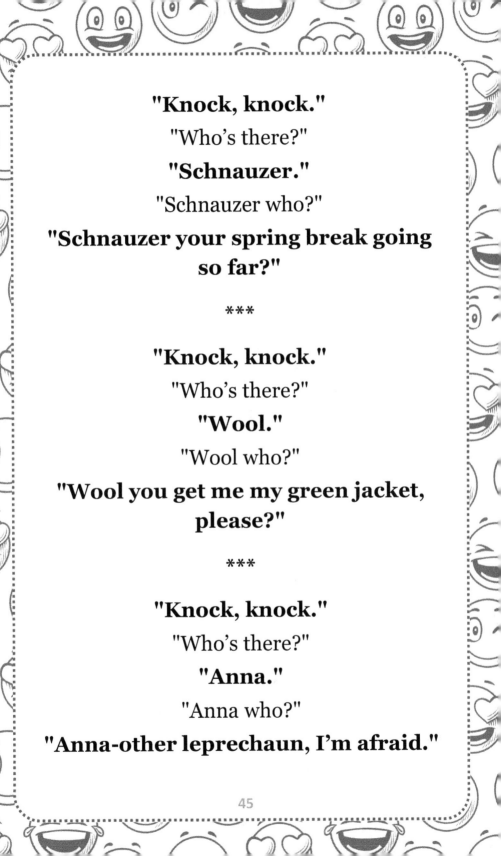

**"Knock, knock."**

"Who's there?"

**"Schnauzer."**

"Schnauzer who?"

**"Schnauzer your spring break going so far?"**

\*\*\*

**"Knock, knock."**

"Who's there?"

**"Wool."**

"Wool who?"

**"Wool you get me my green jacket, please?"**

\*\*\*

**"Knock, knock."**

"Who's there?"

**"Anna."**

"Anna who?"

**"Anna-other leprechaun, I'm afraid."**

**"Knock, knock."**

"Who's there?"

**"Clover."**

"Clover who? "

**"Clover the rainbow, I found a pot of gold!"**

\*\*\*

**"Knock, knock."**

"Who's there?"

**"Riddle."**

"Riddle who?"

**"Riddle me this: Why did the leprechaun sit on the potato? Because it was a couch potato!"**

**"Knock, knock."**

"Who's there?"

**"Stella."**

"Stella who?"

**"Stella-nother leprechaun!"**

\*\*\*

**"Knock, knock."**

"Who's there?"

**"Ray."**

"Ray who?"

**"Rainbows, that's where you can find leprechauns."**

## DID YOU KNOW?

Legend says that there are no snakes in Ireland because St. Patrick banished them with the power of his faith. Nowadays, scientists believe there were never any snakes in Ireland in the first place.

# CHAPTER 4
## April

April obviously opens with April Fools' Day, but it is also when we get Easter: Bunnies, chocolate eggs, and the promise of warmer days. This chapter is full of Easter-related jokes, but also some trickier gags that you can use to prank your friends.

"**Knock, knock.**"

"Who's there?"

"**Heidi.**"

"Heidi who?"

"**Heidi-ing the Easter eggs!**"

# APRIL FOOLS' ANTICS

**"Knock, knock."**
"Who's there?"
**"I came to repair your doorbell."**
"Oh, okay."
**"Just kidding, April Fools'!"**

\*\*\*

**"Knock, knock."**
"Who's there?"
**"Benny."**
"Benny who?"
**"The Easter Benny!"**

**"Knock, knock."**

"Who's there?"

**"No one."**

"No one who?"

***(Don't answer)***

\*\*\*

**"Knock, knock."**

"Who's there?"

**"Bunny."**

"Bunny who?"

**"How many talking bunnies do you know?"**

\*\*\*

**"Knock, knock."**

"Who's there?"

**"Stopwatch."**

"Stopwatch who?"

**"Stopwatch you're doing and let's go Easter egg hunting!"**

**"Knock, knock."**

"Who's there?"

**"Bunny with memory problems!"**

"Bunny with memory problems who?"

**"Knock, knock!"**

\*\*\*

**"Knock, knock."**

"Who's there?"

**"Freddy."**

"Freddy who?"

**"Freddy or not, here I come!"**

**"Knock, knock."**

"Who's there?"

**"Easter."**

"Easter who?"

**"Easter anybody home?"**

\*\*\*

**"Knock, knock."**

"Who's there?"

**"Hatch."**

"Hatch who?"

**"Bless you!"**

**"Knock, knock."**
"Who's there?"
**"Butcher."**
"Butcher who?"
**"Butcher eggs all in the same basket."**

\*\*\*

**"Knock, knock."**
"Who's there?"
**"Bugs."**
"Bugs who?"
**"Bugs Bunny!"**

\*\*\*

**"Knock, knock."**
"Who's there?"
**"Tonto."**
"Tonto who?"
**"Tonto go looking for Easter eggs without me!"**

**"Knock, knock."**

"Who's there?"

**"Kangar."**

"Kangar who?"

**"Nah, mate, I'm the Easter Bunny."**

\*\*\*

**"Knock, knock."**

"Who's there?"

**"Quack."**

"Quack who?"

**"You'll quack those eggs if you drop them."**

**"Knock, knock."**

"Who's there?"

**"Fonda."**

"Fonda who?"

**"Fonda 'nother Easter egg."**

\*\*\*

**"Knock, knock."**

"Who's there?"

**"Boo."**

"Boo who?"

**"Oh, don't cry. It's just a joke!"**

\*\*\*

**"Knock, knock."**

"Who's there?"

**"Some bunny."**

"Some bunny who?"

**"Some bunny stole my chocolate eggs!"**

"Knock, knock."

"Who's there?"

**"Egg."**

"Egg who?"

**"Egg-cited for Easter!"**

\*\*\*

**"Knock, knock."**

"Who's there?"

**"Aslan."**

"Aslan who?"

**"Aslan as you're here, let me tell you a great April Fools' joke..."**

\*\*\*

**"Knock, knock."**

"Who's there?"

**"Easter egg."**

"Easter egg who?"

**"Oh, you crack me up."**

"Knock, knock."

"Who's there?"

**"A little old lady."**

"A little old lady who?"

**"Hey, that's some pretty good yodeling."**

\*\*\*

**"Knock, knock."**

"Who's there?"

**"Bunny."**

"Bunny who?"

**"Bunny the couch, that's where I hid the Easter eggs."**

\*\*\*

**"Knock, knock."**

"Who's there?"

**"Jester."**

"Jester who?"

**"Jesterday was April Fools' Day, but the jokes continue today!"**

**"Knock, knock."**

"Who's there?"

**"Four eggs."**

"Four eggs who?"

**"Four eggs-ample..."**

\*\*\*

**"Knock, knock."**

"Who's there?"

**"Somebody."**

"Somebody who?"

**"Somebody stole your doorbell, that's why I'm knocking."**

**"Knock, knock."**
"Who's there?"
**"Tank."**
"Tank who?"
**"You're welcome. "**

\*\*\*

**"Knock, knock."**
"Who's there?"
**"Esther."**
"Esther who?"
**"Esther Bunny!"**

**"Knock, knock."**

"Who's there?"

**"Noah."**

"Noah who?"

**"Noah body."** *(runs away)*

\*\*\*

**"Knock, knock."**

"Who's there?"

**"Aida."**

"Aida who?"

**"Aida lot of chocolate eggs and now I'm full."**

## DID YOU KNOW?

In Ireland, it is traditional to send people on "fool's errands" as a prank. For instance, one prank involves giving your friend a letter and asking them to deliver it to someone. The letter says only, "Send the fool further," so the person who receives it will ask the poor victim to give the letter to someone else, and so on.

# CHAPTER 5
## May

Spring is definitely here, and so it is time for beautiful flowers, as well as bugs, allergies, and the occasional pouring rain... Yeah, sometimes spring can be not very fun. But it's also time for Mother's Day! Enjoy these flowery jokes.

"Knock, knock."

"Who's there?"

"Betsy."

"Betsy who?"

"Betsy mom in the whole world!"

# SPRING SPRINKLES

**"Knock, knock."**

"Who's there?"

**"Honeydew."**

"Honeydew who?"

**"Honeydew you want to go play in the garden?"**

\*\*\*

**"Knock, knock."**

"Who's there?"

**"Luke."**

"Luke who?"

**"Luke at all these beautiful flowers!"**

**"Knock, knock."**

"Who's there?"

**"Howie."**

"Howie who?"

**"Howie am I supposed to open this umbrella?"**

\*\*\*

**"Knock, knock."**

"Who's there?"

**"Fozzie."**

"Fozzie who?"

**"Fozzie last time, don't step on my petunias!"**

\*\*\*

**"Knock, knock."**

"Who's there?"

**"Tamara."**

"Tamara who?"

**"Tamara is Mother's Day."**

**"Knock, knock."**

"Who's there?"

**"Robin."**

"Robin who?"

**"Robin the neighborhood, spreading springtime cheer!"**

\*\*\*

**"Knock, knock."**

"Who's there?"

**"Blossom."**

"Blossom who?"

**"Blossom with joy, it's springtime!"**

**"Knock, knock."**

"Who's there?"

**"Fanny."**

"Fanny who?"

**"Fanny meeting you here this fine spring morning."**

\*\*\*

**"Knock, knock."**

"Who's there?"

**"Heidi."**

"Heidi who?"

**"Heidi-cided to come play with you in the garden."**

\*\*\*

**"Knock, knock."**

"Who's there?"

**"Darby."**

"Darby who?"

**"Darby many reasons to love your momma."**

**"Knock, knock."**

"Who's there?"

**"Dishes."**

"Dishes who?"

**"Dishes a very nice garden!"**

**\*\*\***

**"Knock, knock."**

"Who's there?"

**"Mom."**

"Mom who?"

**"You don't know who your mom is?"**

**"Knock, knock."**

"Who's there?"

**"Odysseus."**

"Odysseus who?"

**"Odysseus the most beautiful garden I have ever seen."**

\*\*\*

**"Knock, knock."**

"Who's there?"

**"A Fred."**

"A Fred who?"

**"A Fred of allergies this time of year!"**

\*\*\*

**"Knock, knock."**

"Who's there?"

**"Les."**

"Les who?"

**"The Les ants on my garden the better!"**

**"Knock, knock."**

"Who's there?"

**"Acute."**

"Acute who?"

**"Acute gift for Mother's Day."**

\*\*\*

**"Knock, knock."**

"Who's there?"

**"Momma."**

"Momma who?"

**"Mom-magnolias are looking very good this year."**

**"Knock, knock."**

"Who's there?"

**"Poor."**

"Poor who?"

**"Pouring outside!"**

***

**"Knock, knock."**

"Who's there?"

**"Alligator."**

"Alligator who?"

**"Alligator for Mother's Day was this gift card."**

**"Knock, knock."**
"Who's there?"
**"Tickle."**
"Tickle who?"
**"Tickle look at this beautiful garden!"**

\*\*\*

**"Knock, knock."**
"Who's there?"
**"Nougat."**
"Nougat who?"
**"Nougat anything to give your mom for Mother's Day?"**

\*\*\*

**"Knock, knock."**
"Who's there?"
**"Dismay."**
"Dismay who?"
**"Dismay be the most beautiful garden I have ever seen."**

**"Knock, knock."**

"Who's there?"

**"Ohio."**

"Ohio who?"

**"Ohio feeling on this fine spring day?"**

\*\*\*

**"Knock, knock."**

"Who's there?"

**"Razor."**

"Razor who?"

**"Razor hands if you love spring."**

\*\*\*

**"Knock, knock."**

"Who's there?"

**"Warren"**

"Warren who?"

**"Warren you supposed to bring an umbrella?"**

**"Knock, knock."**

"Who's there?"

**"Wilma."**

"Wilma who?"

**"Will Ma like the presents we got for her?"**

\*\*\*

**"Knock, knock."**

"Who's there?"

**"Frank."**

"Frank who?"

**"Frank you for being a great mom!"**

\*\*\*

**"Knock, knock."**

"Who's there?"

**"Dave."**

"Dave who?"

**"Dave walked all over my flowers!"**

**"Knock, knock."**

"Who's there?"

**"Anita."**

"Anita who?"

**"Anita get a gift for Mother's Day!"**

\*\*\*

**"Knock, knock."**

"Who's there?"

**"Arthur."**

"Arthur who?"

**"Arthur any ants in this garden, or can we have a picnic?"**

## DID YOU KNOW?

Besides Mother's Day and Memorial Day, May is also the month when we get *Star Wars* Day! May the Fourth was chosen by *Star Wars* fans to celebrate their favorite space opera franchise so they get to say, "May the Fourth be you."

# CHAPTER 6
## June

Summer is here. Here are some jokes to get your mind off the heat. They're all about camping, the beach, ice cream, and everything else that makes this time nice and relaxing.

"Knock, knock."
"Who's there?"
"Rita."
"Rita who?"
"Rita book during your summer break."

# SUMMER SILLINESS

**"Knock, knock."**
"Who's there?"
**"Sunny."**
"Sunny who?"
**"Sunny out here, isn't it?"**

\*\*\*

**"Knock, knock."**
"Who's there?"
**"Gladys."**
"Gladys who?"
**"Gladys summertime!"**

\*\*\*

**"Knock, knock."**
"Who's there?"
**"Orange."**
"Orange who?"
**"Orange you glad schooltime is over?"**

**"Knock, knock."**
"Who's there?"
**"Canoe."**
"Canoe who?"
**"Canoe open the door, please?"**

*** 

**"Knock, knock."**
"Who's there?"
**"Peach."**
"Peach who?"
**"Peach a tent!"**

*** 

**"Knock, knock."**
"Who's there?"
**"Anita."**
"Anita who?"
**"Anita lift to the beach."**

**"Knock, knock."**

"Who's there?"

**"Banana split."**

"Banana split who?"

**"Banana split, but I'm still here."**

\*\*\*

**"Knock, knock."**

"Who's there?"

**"India."**

"India who?"

**"India summer, we go camping."**

**"Knock, knock."**

"Who's there?"

**"Thermos."**

"Thermos who?"

**"Thermos be a better way to build a tent."**

\*\*\*

**"Knock, knock."**

"Who's there?"

**"Enid."**

"Enid who?"

**"Enid another soda, it's too hot here."**

\*\*\*

**"Knock, knock."**

"Who's there?"

**"Justin."**

"Justin who?"

**"Justin time for a summer adventure!"**

**"Knock, knock."**

"Who's there?"

**"Rose."**

"Rose who?"

**"Rose-ting marshmallows on the campfire.“**

\*\*\*

**"Knock, knock."**

"Who's there?"

**"Donna."**

"Donna who?"

**"Donna give the best Father's Day gifts?"**

**"Knock, knock."**
"Who's there?"
**"Ya."**
"Ya who?"
**"Yeah, I'm also excited for the summer!"**

\*\*\*

**"Knock, knock."**
"Who's there?"
**"Felix."**
"Felix who?"
**"Felix my ice cream, I'll lick his."**

\*\*\*

**"Knock, knock."**
"Who's there?"
**"Hugh."**
"Hugh who?"
**"Yoo-hoo, it's summer!"**

**"Knock, knock."**
"Who's there?"
**"Juno."**
"Juno who?"
**"Juno how hot it is outside?"**

\*\*\*

**"Knock, knock."**
"Who's there?"
**"Alex."**
"Alex who?"
**"Alex-plain the best way to build a campfire."**

\*\*\*

**"Knock, knock."**
"Who's there?"
**"Ears."**
"Ears who?"
**"Ears your Father's Day present!"**

**"Knock, knock."**

"Who's there?"

**"Alpaca."**

"Alpaca who?"

**"Alpaca suitcase for our holidays!"**

***

**"Knock, knock."**

"Who's there?"

**"Tyson."**

"Tyson who?"

**"Tyson rope so we can play beach volleyball."**

***

**"Knock, knock."**

"Who's there?"

**"Icon."**

"Icon who?"

**"Icon put another steak on the grill for you, if you want."**

**"Knock, knock."**

"Who's there?"

**"Tobias."**

"Tobias who?"

**"Tobias cream, we're going to need some money."**

\*\*\*

**"Knock, knock."**

"Who's there?"

**"Amazon."**

"Amazon who?"

**"Amazon of the best dad in the world!"**

\*\*\*

**"Knock, knock."**

"Who's there?"

**"Heatwave."**

"Heatwave who?"

**"Heatwave been waiting for summer to arrive!"**

**"Knock, knock."**

"Who's there?"

**"Wendy."**

"Wendy who?"

**"Wendy you want to go to the beach?"**

\*\*\*

**"Knock, knock."**

"Who's there?"

**"Ben and Anna."**

"Ben and Anna who?"

**"Ben-n'-Anna split."**

\*\*\*

**"Knock, knock."**

"Who's there?"

**"Ice cream."**

"Ice cream who?"

**"Ice cream louder if you want!"**

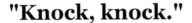

**"Knock, knock."**

"Who's there?"

**"Witches."**

"Witches who?"

**"Witches the fastest way to the beach?"**

## DID YOU KNOW?

There is a species of insect named after the month of June: The June bug, or June beetle, so named because it can only be found in the United States during the months of May and June. Its scientific name, *Phyllophaga*, is Greek for "leaf eaters" because it can cause a lot of damage to the foliage of shrubs and trees.

# CHAPTER 7
## July

Here are some more jokes about the summertime, as well as some more patriotic jokes—appropriate for celebrating the Fourth of July!

"Knock, knock."

"Who's there?"

"Needle."

"Needle who?"

"Needle little more fuel for the barbecue."

# INDEPENDENCE DAY INSANITY

**"Knock, knock."**

"Who's there?"

**"Hugo."**

"Hugo who?"

**"Hugo lit up the grill!"**

\*\*\*

**"Knock, knock."**

"Who's there?"

**"Barbie."**

"Barbie who?"

**"Barbie-cue is ready to be fired up."**

\*\*\*

**"Knock, knock."**

"Who's there?"

**"Grate."**

"Grate who?"

**"Grate job on firing up the grill, chef!"**

**"Knock, knock."**
"Who's there?"
**"Hippo."**
"Hippo who?"
**"Hippo Fourth of July!"**

\*\*\*

**"Knock, knock."**
"Who's there?"
**"Imogen."**
"Imogen who?"
**"Imogen how much fun we're going to have this summer!"**

\*\*\*

**"Knock, knock."**
"Who's there?"
**"Ford."**
"Ford who?"
**"Ford of July!"**

**"Knock, knock."**
"Who's there?"
**"Jan."**
"Jan who?"
**"Jan-kee Doodle!"**

\*\*\*

**"Knock, knock."**
"Who's there?"
**"Tarzan."**
"Tarzan who?"
**"Tarzan stripes forever!"**

\*\*\*

**"Knock, knock."**
"Who's there?"
**"Jimmy."**
"Jimmy who?"
**"Jimmy another burger!"**

**"Knock, knock."**

"Who's there?"

**"Martini."**

"Martini who?"

**"Martini swim shorts don't fit anymore."**

***

**"Knock, knock."**

"Who's there?"

**"Toronto."**

"Toronto who?"

**"Toronto be a law against rain on the Fourth of July!"**

**"Knock, knock."**

"Who's there?"

**"Bert."**

"Bert who?"

**"Bert the meat on the barbecue."**

\*\*\*

**"Knock, knock."**

"Who's there?"

**"Gus."**

"Gus who?"

**"Gus how many fireworks we saw yesterday."**

\*\*\*

**"Knock, knock."**

"Who's there?"

**"Possum."**

"Possum who?"

**"Possum burgers on the barbecue!"**

**"Knock, knock."**

"Who's there?"

**"Thyme."**

"Thyme who?"

**"Thyme for some fireworks!"**

\*\*\*

**"Knock, knock."**

"Who's there?"

**"Gorilla."**

"Gorilla who?"

**"Gorilla me a burger, I'm starving."**

\*\*\*

**"Knock, knock."**

"Who's there?"

**"Sauce."**

"Sauce who?"

**"Sauce me the ribs, it's time to get saucy at the grill!"**

**"Knock, knock."**
"Who's there?"
**"Rose."**
"Rose who?"
**"Rose some chicken on the barbecue."**

\*\*\*

**"Knock, knock."**
"Who's there?"
**"Iguana."**
"Iguana who?"
**"Iguana watch the fireworks with you."**

\*\*\*

**"Knock, knock."**
"Who's there?"
**"Police."**
"Police who?"
**"Police hurry and open the door, it's really hot outside."**

**"Knock, knock."**
"Who's there?"
**"Halibut."**
"Halibut who?"
**"Halibut some burgers?"**

\*\*\*

**"Knock, knock."**
"Who's there?"
**"Grover."**
"Grover who?"
**"Grover here and give me a hand with this barbecue."**

\*\*\*

**"Knock, knock."**
"Who's there?"
**"Barbecue."**
"Barbecue who?"
**"Barb-be-cute, but you be cuter."**

**"Knock, knock."**

"Who's there?"

**"Butter."**

"Butter who?"

**"Butter stand back, I just lit the fuse on these fireworks!"**

\*\*\*

**"Knock, knock."**

"Who's there?"

**"Matty."**

"Matty who?"

**"Matty nice of you to invite me to your barbecue."**

\*\*\*

**"Knock, knock."**

"Who's there?"

**"Butch."**

"Butch who?"

**"Butch some meat on the grill, we're hungry!"**

**"Knock, knock."**

"Who's there?"

**"Bjorn."**

"Bjorn who?"

**"Bjorn in the USA!"**

\*\*\*

**"Knock, knock."**

"Who's there?"

**"Denise."**

"Denise who?"

**"Denise, the nephews, the cousins, they're all here for the party!"**

\*\*\*

**"Knock, knock."**

"Who's there?"

**"Warner."**

"Warner who?"

**"Warner go watch the fireworks?"**

**"Knock, knock."**

"Who's there?"

**"Feather."**

"Feather who?"

**"Feather last time, will you fire up the grill?"**

### DID YOU KNOW?

The ancient Romans used a calendar with only 10 months before Julius Caesar introduced a new calendar with 12 months, very similar to the one we use today. We call it the Julian calendar in honor of its creator, and one of the new months, July, is also named after Julius.

# CHAPTER 8
## August

Summer is almost over, and so it's time to go back to school! Enjoy this backpack full of gags!

"Knock, knock."
"Who's there?"
"Harvey."
"Harvey who?"
**"Harvey good day at school!"**

# BACK TO SCHOOL BANTER

**"Knock, knock."**

"Who's there?"

**"Phil."**

"Phil who?"

**"Phil-ling my backpack with books."**

***

**"Knock, knock."**

"Who's there?"

**"Abe."**

"Abe who?"

**"Abe, C, D, E, F, G..."**

***

**"Knock, knock."**

"Who's there?"

**"Eyesore."**

"Eyesore who?"

**"Eyesore love coming back to school!"**

**"Knock, knock."**

"Who's there?"

**"Needle."**

"Needle who?"

**"Needle little help finding my classroom."**

***

**"Knock, knock."**

"Who's there?"

**"Water."**

"Water who?"

**"Water you mean, it's time to go back to school?"**

***

**"Knock, knock."**

"Who's there?"

**"Hubie."**

"Hubie who?"

**"Hubie-ginning school tomorrow?"**

**"Knock, knock."**

"Who's there?"

**"Ike."**

"Ike who?"

**"Ike-an't believe we have to go to school tomorrow."**

*\*\*\**

**"Knock, knock."**

"Who's there?"

**"Viola."**

"Viola who?"

**"Viola these crayons in your backpack?"**

*\*\*\**

**"Knock, knock."**

"Who's there?"

**"York."**

"York who?"

**"York coming to school today, right?"**

**"Knock, knock."**

"Who's there?"

**"Gander."**

"Gander who?"

**"Gander teacher come help me with this work?"**

\*\*\*

**"Knock, knock."**

"Who's there?"

**"Oscar."**

"Oscar who?"

**"Oscar the teacher if you have any questions."**

**"Knock, knock."**

"Who's there?"

**"Joe King."**

"Joe King who?"

**"Joe King around before we have to go to class."**

***

**"Knock, knock."**

"Who's there?"

**"Keanu."**

"Keanu who?"

**"Keanu believe it's already time to go back to school?"**

***

**"Knock, knock."**

"Who's there?"

**"Lunchtime."**

"Lunchtime who?'

**"Lunchtime is the only subject I never skip!"**

**"Knock, knock."**

"Who's there?"

**"Guinevere."**

"Guinevere who?"

**"Guinevere going back to class?"**

\*\*\*

**"Knock, knock."**

"Who's there?"

**"Leaf."**

"Leaf who?"

**"Leaf me alone, I'm trying to study."**

\*\*\*

**"Knock, knock."**

"Who's there?"

**"Broken pencil."**

"Broken pencil who?"

**"Never mind, it's pointless."**

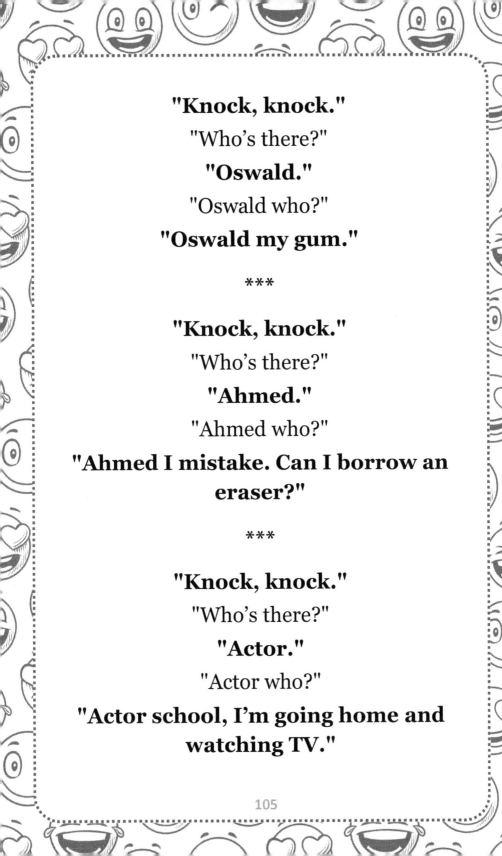

**"Knock, knock."**

"Who's there?"

**"Oswald."**

"Oswald who?"

**"Oswald my gum."**

\*\*\*

**"Knock, knock."**

"Who's there?"

**"Ahmed."**

"Ahmed who?"

**"Ahmed I mistake. Can I borrow an eraser?"**

\*\*\*

**"Knock, knock."**

"Who's there?"

**"Actor."**

"Actor who?"

**"Actor school, I'm going home and watching TV."**

**"Knock, knock."**

"Who's there?"

**"Pencil."**

"Pencil who?"

**"Pencil fall down if you don't wear a belt! "**

\*\*\*

**"Knock, knock."**

"Who's there?"

**"Owl."**

"Owl who?"

**"Owl always remember the good times we had in school!"**

\*\*\*

**"Knock, knock."**

"Who's there?"

**"Spell."**

"Spell who?"

**"W-H-O."**

**"Knock, knock."**
"Who's there?"
**"Otto."**
"Otto who?"
**"Autumn is what they call Fall in England."**

\*\*\*

**"Knock, knock."**
"Who's there?"
**"Althea."**
"Althea who?"
**"Althea after school!"**

\*\*\*

**"Knock, knock."**
"Who's there?"
**"Harry."**
"Harry who?"
**"Harry up, we got to go to school!"**

**"Knock, knock."**

"Who's there?"

**"Alaska."**

"Alaska who?"

**"Alaska the teacher, I don't understand this exercise."**

***

**"Knock, knock."**

"Who's there?"

**"To."**

"To who?"

**"It's actually 'to whom.'"**

***

**"Knock, knock."**

"Who's there?"

**"George Washington."**

"George Washington who?"

**"You don't know who George Washington is? You really should be in school!"**

**"Knock, knock."**

"Who's there?"

**"Woo."**

"Woo hoo?"

**"Yeah, I'm excited to go back to school too!"**

## DID YOU KNOW?

In America, August is National Sandwich Month. Sandwiches were supposedly invented by—and named after—the Earl of Sandwich in August of 1762. Legend says that the Earl wanted to eat meat while playing cards, so he needed a way to eat without a knife and fork and without getting his hands greasy. Somebody—either the Earl himself or his personal cook—had the brilliant idea of just putting the meat between two pieces of toasted bread.

# CHAPTER 9
## September

September is time for the harvest—fruits and vegetables are ripe for picking, and so are these jokes.

"**Knock, knock.**"
"Who's there?"
"**Seth.**"
"Seth who?"
"**Seth-tember First!**"

# HARVEST HILARITY

**"Knock, knock."**
"Who's there?"
**"Cash."**
"Cash who?"
**"No thanks, I prefer almonds."**

\*\*\*

**"Knock, knock."**
"Who's there?"
**"Beets."**
"Beets who?"
**"Beets me!"**

\*\*\*

**"Knock, knock."**
"Who's there?"
**"Alva."**
"Alva who?"
**"Alva 'nother apple, please."**

**"Knock, knock."**

"Who's there?"

**"Bison."**

"Bison who?"

**"Bison fresh produce from my farm!"**

\*\*\*

**"Knock, knock."**

"Who's there?"

**"Lay."**

"Lay who?"

**"Lay-bor Day is almost here!"**

**"Knock, knock."**

"Who's there?"

**"Pete."**

"Pete who?"

**"Pete-riot's Day is almost here too."**

***

**"Knock, knock."**

"Who's there?"

**"Carmen."**

"Carmen who?"

**"Carmen get it, this pie is fresh from the oven."**

***

**"Knock, knock."**

"Who's there?"

**"Cantina."**

"Cantina who?"

**"Can Tina come out to pick apples with us?"**

"Knock, knock."

"Who's there?"

"Juan."

"Juan who?"

"Juan more slice of pie, please."

\*\*\*

"Knock, knock."

"Who's there?"

"Pumpkin."

"Pumpkin who?"

"Pumpkin pie is great this time of year."

\*\*\*

"Knock, knock."

"Who's there?"

"Cucumber."

"Cucumber who?"

"Since when do cucumbers have last names?"

**"Knock, knock."**

"Who's there?"

**"Crispin."**

"Crispin who?"

**"Crispin savory, those are the best apples."**

\*\*\*

**"Knock, knock."**

"Who's there?"

**"Bean."**

"Bean who?"

**"Bean a while since we had such a good harvest."**

**"Knock, knock."**

"Who's there?"

**"Abbott."**

"Abbot who?"

**"Abbott time you came to help us pick fruit."**

\*\*\*

**"Knock, knock."**

"Who's there?"

**"Corn."**

"Corn who?"

**"Corn-gratulations on a fruitful harvest!"**

\*\*\*

**"Knock, knock."**

"Who's there?"

**"Tom."**

"Tom who?"

**"Tomato-picking is lots of fun!"**

**"Knock, knock."**
"Who's there?"
**"Dee."**
"Dee who?"
**"Dee-licious produce grown locally!"**

\*\*\*

**"Knock, knock."**
"Who's there?"
**"Juicy."**
"Juicy who?"
**"Juicy what I see? Look at all this produce!"**

\*\*\*

**"Knock, knock."**
"Who's there?"
**"Lettuce."**
"Lettuce who?"
**"Lettuce in, we brought food!"**

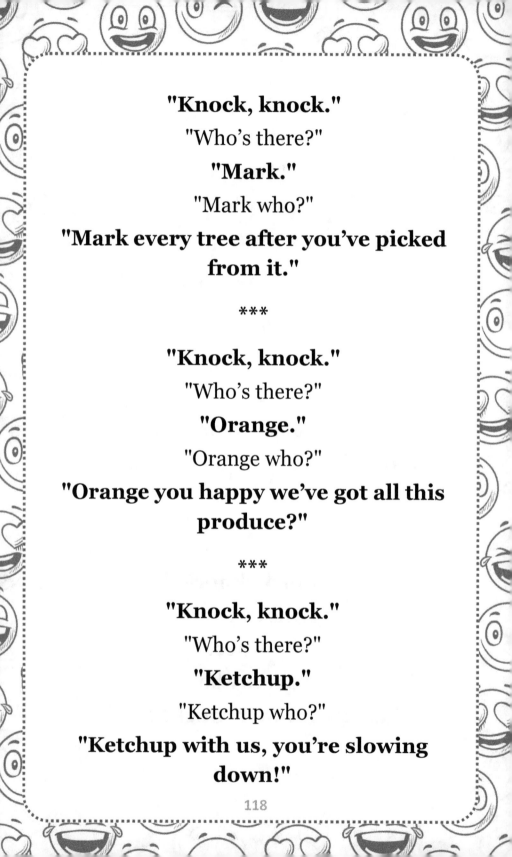

"Knock, knock."

"Who's there?"

**"Mark."**

"Mark who?"

**"Mark every tree after you've picked from it."**

\*\*\*

"Knock, knock."

"Who's there?"

**"Orange."**

"Orange who?"

**"Orange you happy we've got all this produce?"**

\*\*\*

"Knock, knock."

"Who's there?"

**"Ketchup."**

"Ketchup who?"

**"Ketchup with us, you're slowing down!"**

**"Knock, knock."**

"Who's there?"

**"Wine."**

"Wine who?"

**"Wine don't you like this food I cooked for you?"**

\*\*\*

**"Knock, knock."**

"Who's there?"

**"Donut."**

"Donut who?"

**"Donut worry, it's almost Halloween!"**

**"Knock, knock."**

"Who's there?"

**"Butter."**

"Butter who?"

**"Butter open quick, I brought you some pie!"**

\*\*\*

**"Knock, knock."**

"Who's there?"

**"Don."**

"Don who?"

**"Don' wear white socks after Labor Day."**

\*\*\*

**"Knock, knock."**

"Who's there?"

**"Aida."**

"Aida who?"

**"Aida loved going apple picking with you."**

**"Knock, knock."**

"Who's there?"

**"Musket."**

"Musket who?"

**"Musket be September, I can smell pumpkin spice!"**

\*\*\*

**"Knock, knock."**

"Who's there?"

**"Al."**

"Al who?"

**"Al-most October!"**

## DID YOU KNOW?

September 19 is International Talk Like a Pirate Day: A day when everyone, both kids and grownups, are encouraged to talk like a pirate, shout "Arrr!" and say pirate things like, "Walk the plank, matey!"

# CHAPTER 10
## October

The spookiest month asks for the spookiest jokes. Be warned, all ye who knock on this door: These gags are not for the easily frightened.

"Knock, knock."
"Who's there?"
"Your kin."
"My kin who?"
"Your pumpkin, of course."

# HALLOWEEN HOWLERS

**"Knock, knock."**

"Who's there?"

**"Howl."**

"Howl who?"

**"Howl you know unless you open the door? "**

\*\*\*

**"Knock, knock."**

"Who's there?"

**"Witch."**

"Witch who?"

**"Witch way to the Halloween party?"**

\*\*\*

**"Knock, knock."**

"Who's there?"

**"Disappearing ghost."**

"Disappearing ghost who?"

***(Don't answer)***

"Knock, knock."

"Who's there?"

"Ghouly."

"Ghouly who?"

"That's right: Ghouly-who Iglesias, the famous singer."

\*\*\*

"Knock, knock."

"Who's there?"

"Alma."

"Alma who?"

"Alma-ny pumpkins should we carve this year?"

\*\*\*

"Knock, knock."

"Who's there?"

"Zack."

"Zack who?"

"Zack full of candy I got from trick-or-treating!"

**"Knock, knock."**

"Who's there?"

**"Candy."**

"Candy who?"

**"Candy grownups give me a hand with my Halloween costume?"**

\*\*\*

**"Knock, knock."**

"Who's there?"

**"Celeste."**

"Celeste who?"

**"Celeste time I'm going trick-or-treating with you! "**

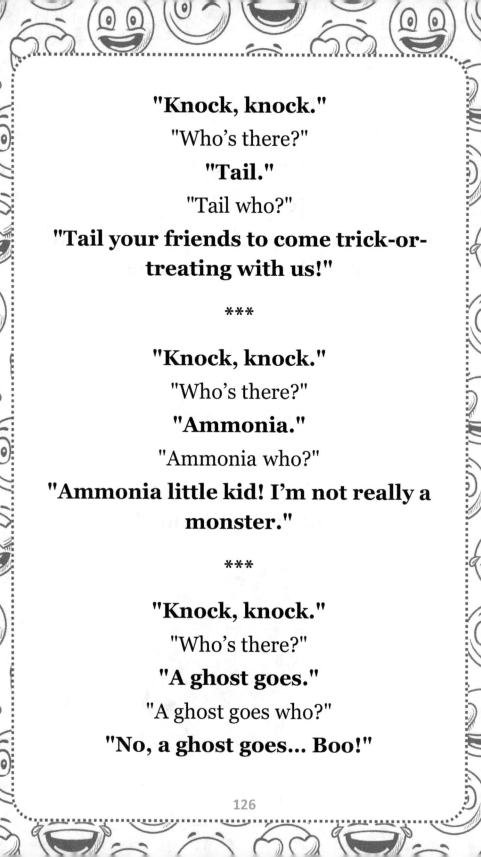

**"Knock, knock."**

"Who's there?"

**"Tail."**

"Tail who?"

**"Tail your friends to come trick-or-treating with us!"**

\*\*\*

**"Knock, knock."**

"Who's there?"

**"Ammonia."**

"Ammonia who?"

**"Ammonia little kid! I'm not really a monster."**

\*\*\*

**"Knock, knock."**

"Who's there?"

**"A ghost goes."**

"A ghost goes who?"

**"No, a ghost goes... Boo!"**

**"Knock, knock."**

"Who's there?"

**"Manny."**

"Manny who?"

**"Manny wicked things are going to happen tonight..."**

\*\*\*

**"Knock, knock."**

"Who's there?"

**"Holly."**

"Holly who?"

**"Holly-ween!"**

\*\*\*

**"Knock, knock."**

"Who's there?"

**"Trish."**

"Trish who?"

**"Trish or Treat!"**

"Knock, knock."

"Who's there?"

**"Maia."**

"Maia who?"

**"Maia outfit got stuck on the door."**

\*\*\*

**"Knock, knock."**

"Who's there?"

**"Bethany."**

"Bethany who?"

**"Bethany good scary movies recently?"**

\*\*\*

**"Knock, knock."**

"Who's there?"

**"Ghost."**

"Ghost who?"

**"Ghost-a la vista, baby! It's Halloween!"**

**"Knock, knock."**

"Who's there?"

**"Scott."**

"Scott who?"

**"Scott to be a better way to get candy than this."**

\*\*\*

**"Knock, knock."**

"Who's there?"

**"Vampire."**

"Vampire who?"

**"Vampire Strikes Back!"**

\*\*\*

**"Knock, knock."**

"Who's there?"

**"Turin."**

"Turin who?"

**"Turin into a vampire!"**

"Knock, knock."

"Who's there?"

**"Lego."**

"Lego who?"

**"Lego trick-or-treating!"**

\*\*\*

"Knock, knock."

"Who's there?"

**"Yoda."**

"Yoda who?"

**"Yoda one who chose this Halloween costume."**

\*\*\*

"Knock, knock."

"Who's there?"

**"Gino."**

"Gino who?"

**"Gino I'm too scared to go out at night."**

**"Knock, knock."**

"Who's there?"

**"Senior."**

"Senior who?"

**"Senior Halloween costume and I'm very impressed."**

***

**"Knock, knock."**

"Who's there?"

**"Disguise."**

"Disguise who?"

**"Disguise are here to ask you for candy."**

**"Knock, knock."**

"Who's there?"

**"It's Pasture."**

"It's Pasture who?"

**"It's Pasture bedtime. Go to bed!"**

\*\*\*

**"Knock, knock."**

"Who's there?"

**"Witch."**

"Witch who?"

**"Witch one of you is going to let me in?"**

\*\*\*

**"Knock, knock."**

"Who's there?"

**"Howie."**

"Howie who?"

**"Howie am I supposed to walk around in this ridiculous costume?"**

**"Knock, knock."**

"Who's there?"

**"Tad."**

"Tad who?"

**"Tad kid just stole all our candy!"**

\*\*\*

**"Knock, knock."**

"Who's there?"

**"Han."**

"Han who?"

**"Han-ted House!"**

## DID YOU KNOW?

Famous people born on Halloween include American astronaut Michael Collins, comedy actors John Candy and Rob Schneider, director Peter Jackson, singer Willow Smith, and the Gorillaz character Noodle.

# CHAPTER 11
## November

The spookiest month asks for the spookiest jokes. Be warned, all ye who knock on this door: These gags are not for the easily frightened.

"Knock, knock."

"Who's there?"

"Turkeys."

"Turkeys who?"

"No, turkeys gobble. It's owls that go 'who.'"

# THANKSGIVING TIDINGS

**"Knock, knock."**

"Who's there?"

**"Possum."**

"Possum who?"

**"Possum gravy on the potatoes."**

\*\*\*

**"Knock, knock."**

"Who's there?"

**"Ava."**

"Ava who?"

**"Ava had too much turkey."**

\*\*\*

**"Knock, knock."**

"Who's there?"

**"Sid."**

"Sid who?"

**"Sid down, it's time for dinner."**

"Knock, knock."

"Who's there?"

**"Ken."**

"Ken who?"

**"Ken you pass the mashed potatoes, please?"**

\*\*\*

"Knock, knock."

"Who's there?"

**"Turkey."**

"Turkey who?"

**"Turn-the-key to open the door."**

\*\*\*

"Knock, knock."

"Who's there?"

**"Xavier."**

"Xavier who?"

**"Xavier appetite, it's almost time for dinner."**

**"Knock, knock."**

"Who's there?"

**"Coal."**

"Coal who?"

**"Coal me when it's time for dinner."**

\*\*\*

**"Knock, knock."**

"Who's there?"

**"Gravy."**

"Gravy who?"

**"Gravy-ting you with a smile on this Thanksgiving Day!"**

\*\*\*

**"Knock, knock."**

"Who's there?"

**"Esther."**

"Esther who?"

**"Esther any more pie?"**

**"Knock, knock."**

"Who's there?"

**"Heaven."**

"Heaven who?"

**"Heaven seen you since last year's Thanksgiving!"**

**\*\*\***

**"Knock, knock."**

"Who's there?"

**"Gray."**

"Gray who?"

**"Gray-vy boat!"**

**"Knock, knock."**

"Who's there?"

**"Seth."**

"Seth who?"

**"Seth the table, it's almost time for dinner."**

\*\*\*

**"Knock, knock."**

"Who's there?"

**"Don."**

"Don who?"

**"Don' eat all the mashed potatoes, leave some for us."**

\*\*\*

**"Knock, knock."**

"Who's there?"

**"Stopwatch."**

"Stopwatch who?"

**"Stopwatch you're doing, it's time for Thanksgiving dinner."**

**"Knock, knock."**

"Who's there?"

**"Cookie."**

"Cookie who?"

**"Cooking Thanksgiving dinner!"**

\*\*\*

**"Knock, knock."**

"Who's there?"

**"Gobble gobble."**

"Gobble gobble who?"

**"You sound like a turkey trying to be an owl."**

\*\*\*

**"Knock, knock."**

"Who's there?"

**"Bacon."**

"Bacon who?"

**"Bacon a delicious pumpkin pie."**

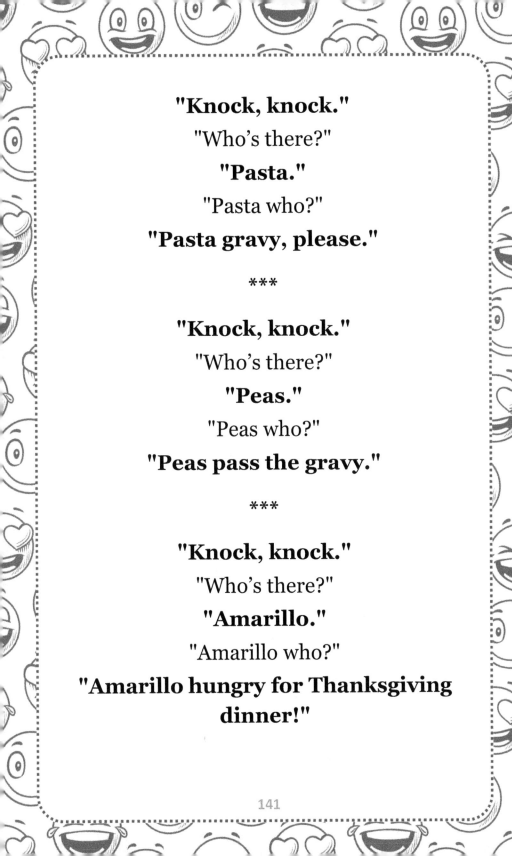

**"Knock, knock."**
"Who's there?"
**"Pasta."**
"Pasta who?"
**"Pasta gravy, please."**

\*\*\*

**"Knock, knock."**
"Who's there?"
**"Peas."**
"Peas who?"
**"Peas pass the gravy."**

\*\*\*

**"Knock, knock."**
"Who's there?"
**"Amarillo."**
"Amarillo who?"
**"Amarillo hungry for Thanksgiving dinner!"**

**"Knock, knock."**

"Who's there?"

**"Closure."**

"Closure who?"

**"Closure mouth when you chew."**

\*\*\*

**"Knock, knock."**

"Who's there?"

**"Huge."**

"Huge who?"

**"Hu-just in time for dinner!"**

**"Knock, knock."**

"Who's there?"

**"Peas."**

"Peas who? "

**"Peas and love to you."**

\*\*\*

**"Knock, knock."**

"Who's there?"

**"Pecan."**

"Pecan who?"

**"Pecan somebody your own size!"**

\*\*\*

**"Knock, knock."**

"Who's there?"

**"Tomato."**

"Tomato who?"

**"Tom ate all the pie and didn't leave any for us."**

**"Knock, knock."**

"Who's there?"

**"Armageddon."**

"Armageddon who?"

**"Armageddon another slice of pie?"**

\*\*\*

**"Knock, knock."**

"Who's there?"

**"Annie."**

"Annie who?"

**"Annie body want some leftovers?"**

\*\*\*

**"Knock, knock."**

"Who's there?"

**"Henriette."**

"Henriette who?"

**"Henriette all the turkey and two slices of pumpkin pie!"**

**"Knock, knock."**

"Who's there?"

**"Bill."**

"Bill who?"

**"Bill-grims coming for Thanksgiving dinner!"**

## DID YOU KNOW?

The first Thanksgiving was celebrated in 1621 by the Pilgrims and the people of the Wampanoag tribe. Historians believe that they ate goose, duck, swan, fish, and even deer, but probably not turkey. Eating turkey on Thanksgiving didn't become a tradition until later.

# CHAPTER 12
## December

No matter what you celebrate this time of year, December is a time for people to remind each other of what is really important. It may be cold outside, but at least we're together. So when someone comes knocking at your door, make sure to let them in—whether they're carol singers or the jolly fat man himself.

**"Knock, knock."**
"Who's there?"
**"Turnip."**
"Turnip who?"
**"Turnip the volume, I love listening to holiday songs!"**

# HOLIDAY HILARITY

**"Knock, knock."**

"Who's there?"

**"Dre."**

"Dre who?"

**"Dreidel, dreidel, dreidel, I made you out of clay..."**

\*\*\*

**"Knock, knock."**

"Who's there?"

**"Rude."**

"Rude who?"

**"Rude-olph, the Red-Nosed Reindeer."**

\*\*\*

**"Knock, knock."**

"Who's there?"

**"Ginger."**

"Ginger who?"

**"Gingerbread Man!"**

**"Knock, knock."**

"Who's there?"

**"Reindeer."**

"Reindeer who?"

**"Rain, dear. Get an umbrella!"**

\*\*\*

**"Knock, knock."**

"Who's there?"

**"Hosanna."**

"Hosanna who?"

**"Hosanna Claus going to enter? We don't have a chimney."**

**"Knock, knock."**

"Who's there?"

**"Tree."**

"Tree who?"

**"Tree Wise Men!"**

\*\*\*

**"Knock, knock."**

"Who's there?"

**"Elf."**

"Elf who?"

**"Elf I knock louder, will you let me in?"**

\*\*\*

**"Knock, knock."**

"Who's there?"

**"Honda."**

"Honda who?"

**"Honda first day of Christmas, my true love gave to me..."**

"Knock, knock."

"Who's there?"

"Hannah."

"Hannah who?"

"Hannah-kah is almost here!"

\*\*\*

"Knock, knock."

"Who's there?"

"Harold."

"Harold who?"

"Hark the Harold angels sing..."

\*\*\*

"Knock, knock."

"Who's there?"

"Holly."

"Holly who?"

"Holly-day season!"

**"Knock, knock."**

"Who's there?"

**"Avery."**

"Avery who?"

**"Avery Merry Christmas!"**

**\*\*\***

**"Knock, knock."**

"Who's there?"

**"Santa."**

"Santa who?"

**"Well, you don't have a chimney, so I had to knock on the door."**

**"Knock, knock."**

"Who's there?"

**"Alex."**

"Alex who?"

**"Alex Santa for a new bike for Christmas!"**

\*\*\*

**"Knock, knock."**

"Who's there?"

**"Mary."**

"Mary who?"

**"Merry Christmas!"**

\*\*\*

**"Knock, knock."**

"Who's there?"

**"Chris."**

"Chris who?"

**"Christmas tidings!"**

**"Knock, knock."**

"Who's there?"

**"Water."**

"Water who?"

**"Water you doing for Kwanzaa this year?"**

***

**"Knock, knock."**

"Who's there?"

**"Dexter."**

"Dexter who?"

**"Dexter hall with boughs of holly..."**

***

**"Knock, knock."**

"Who's there?"

**"Claus."**

"Claus who?"

**"Claus that's how the joke goes!"**

**"Knock, knock."**
"Who's there?"
**"Ho, ho, ho!"**
"Ho, ho, ho, who?"
**"Who else do you know who laughs like this?"**

\*\*\*

**"Knock, knock."**
"Who's there?"
**"Olive."**
"Olive who?"
**"Olive the Other Reindeer!"**

\*\*\*

**"Knock, knock."**
"Who's there?"
**"Ho, ho."**
"Ho, ho, who?"
**"You have to work on your Santa impression."**

**"Knock, knock."**

"Who's there?"

**"Anna."**

"Anna who?"

**"Anna partridge in a pear tree!"**

\*\*\*

**"Knock, knock."**

"Who's there?"

**"Elf."**

"Elf who?"

**"Elf-abet: A, B, C, D, E..."**

\*\*\*

**"Knock, knock."**

"Who's there?"

**"Yule log."**

"Yule log who?"

**"Yule log the door after I come in, won't you?"**

**"Knock, knock."**

"Who's there?"

**"Santa."**

"Santa who?"

**"Santa text saying I would be here. Did you get it?"**

\*\*\*

**"Knock, knock."**

"Who's there?"

**"Abby and Hannah."**

"Abby and Hannah who?"

**"Abby Christmas, Hannah Happy New Year!"**

\*\*\*

**"Knock, knock."**

"Who's there?"

**"Snow."**

"Snow who?"

**"Snow use trying to hide, Santa knows if you've been naughty or nice!"**

**"Knock, knock."**

"Who's there?"

**"Gift."**

"Gift who?"

**"Gift me a big smile, it's Christmas Day!"**

\*\*\*

**"Knock, knock."**

"Who's there?"

**"Donut."**

"Donut who?"

**"Donut open until Christmas."**

## DID YOU KNOW?

In the 1980s, KFC ran a campaign that told the Japanese people that eating fried chicken could be their first Yuletide tradition since they didn't have any. The campaign was so successful that nowadays if you live in Japan, you have to make a reservation at KFC several months in advance if you want to eat there on Christmas Day.

# CONCLUSION

Knock, knock.

Who's there?

Thank you.

Thank you who?

Thank you for reading our book! We hope we gave you enough chuckles to last for a whole year, and we hope we inspired you to make up your own knock-knock jokes! It's fun!

If you've enjoyed this book, we would greatly appreciate your support in leaving a review on our product page.

Keep the laughs flowing—and for Pete's sake, get your doorbell fixed!

# REFERENCES

Haggerty, B. (n.d.). *April Fool's Day.* Irish Culture and Customs. Retrieved April 22, 2023, from https://www.irishcultureandcustoms.com/ACale nd/AprilFools.html

*International talk like a pirate day.* (n.d.). Wikipedia. Retrieved April 22, 2023, from https://en.wikipedia.org/wiki/International_Tal k_Like_a_Pirate_Day

*Julian calendar.* (n.d.). Wikipedia. Retrieved April 22, 2023, from https://en.wikipedia.org/wiki/Julian_calendar

*Knock knock jokes.* (n.d.). Knock Knock Jokes. Retrieved April 20, 2023, from https://www.knockknockjokes.nu/

*Knock-knock jokes: The best knock-knock jokes.* (n.d.). Reader's Digest. Retrieved April 19, 2023, from https://www.rd.com/jokes/knock-knock/

*Phyllophaga.* (n.d.). Wikipedia. Retrieved April 22, 2023, from https://en.wikipedia.org/wiki/Phyllophaga

*Sandwich.* (n.d.). Wikipedia. Retrieved April 22, 2023, from https://en.wikipedia.org/wiki/Sandwich